Why is Mary looking so startled? Join up the dots to find out.
Who gives Mary a surprise visit?
You can find this story in Luke 1:26–38.

1

Mary lived in the village of Nazareth. The angel Gabriel visited Mary to tell her she was going to have a baby boy. The artist has made lots of deliberate mistakes. How many can you find?
You can read this story in Luke 1:26–38.

Mary was astonished when the angel Gabriel told her she would have a very special baby son, Jesus. Can you find twelve brooms hidden in this picture?
Look up the story of the angel's visit in Luke 1:26–38.

Here's another illustration of the angel Gabriel telling Mary she will have a special baby. Can you find all the silly mistakes the artist has made? *Read Luke 1:26–38.*

Mary's cousin Elizabeth had a baby around the same time. When the boy was born, Elizabeth's husband couldn't speak, so he wrote the baby's name. It was "John". Can you find all the deliberate mistakes in this picture? *Read Luke 1:57–66.*

God said that Elizabeth's son should be called John.
Can you find all twelve pencils hidden in this picture?
Look up the story of the birth of Elizabeth's son, John, in Luke 1:57–66.

Joseph was engaged to Mary. An angel told him in a dream that God was giving Mary a special baby boy. How many rings can you find hidden here?
Read Matthew 1:18–25.

God told Mary to marry Joseph. What is Joseph doing here?
Join up the dots to find out!
Read about Joseph and Mary in Luke 2:1–7.

Mary's husband, Joseph, was a carpenter.
Can you find ten differences between these two pictures of Joseph hammering in his workshop?
Read Matthew 13:55.

Mary married Joseph, the carpenter in Nazareth.
Can you find all the mistakes in this picture of Joseph's workshop?
Read more about Joseph in Matthew 1:19–24.

It was nearly time for Jesus to be born. But Mary and Joseph had to go on a long journey.
Help them to find the right road. *You can read this story in Luke 2:1–5.*
What is the name of the place where they are going? Write it on the puzzle.

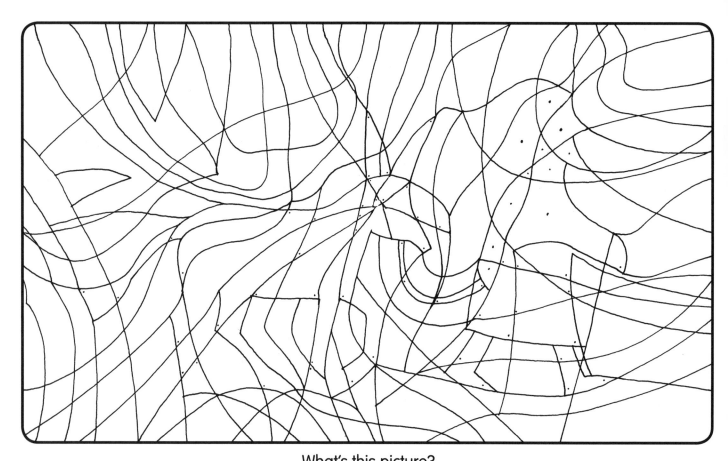

What's this picture?
Fill in all the shapes that have a dot in them to find out what the artist has hidden.
Read the story of Joseph and Mary's journey in Luke 2:1–7.

Joseph is leading his donkey to the town of Bethlehem.
Which two pictures are *exactly* the same?
Read the story in Luke 2:1–7.

Mary and Joseph journeyed to Bethlehem. Why did they have to go there?
Can you find all the deliberate mistakes in this picture?
You can read about this in Luke 2:1–7.

Mary and Joseph are arriving somewhere.
Join up the dots to discover what they see.
You can find this story in Luke 2:1–5.

15

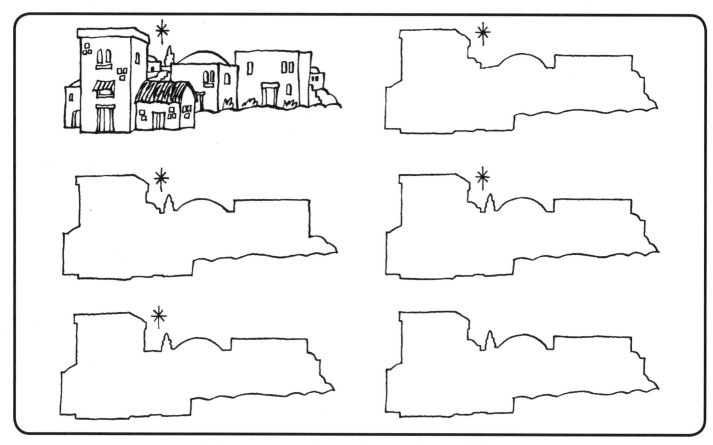

At last Mary and Joseph arrived in Bethlehem.
Which outline exactly fits the picture of Bethlehem?
Read this story in Luke 2:4–7.

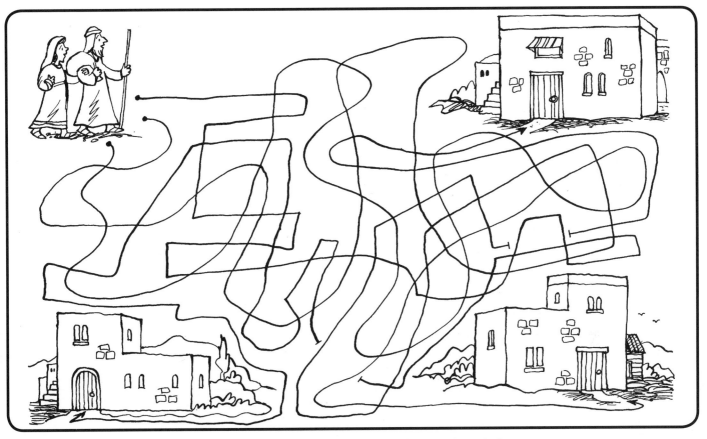

At which inn in Bethlehem did Mary and Joseph ask for a room?
Follow the lines to find out.
Read the story in Luke 2:6–7.

Join up the dots to finish this picture.
The innkeeper said to Mary and Joseph, "I have no r_ _ _ for you."
You can find this story in Luke 2:6–7.

Mary and Joseph arrive at the inn. Does the man have a room for them?
Complete the drawings of the other houses in Bethlehem. Add windows and doors.
Read about this in Luke 2:6–7.

Joseph and Mary discovered there was no room for them at the inn.
You can read about this in Luke 2:7. Complete this picture of the stable where Jesus was born.
Which animals might be in the stable?

Join up the dots to complete the picture.
What did Mary use as a cot for little baby Jesus?
You can find this story in Luke 2:7.

21

Jesus is born in the Bethlehem stable.
Can you find the ten lanterns that the artist has hidden in the stable?
Read this story in Luke 2:1–7.

In the stable where Jesus was born there were probably cows and a donkey.
Which box has all the pieces needed to make the complete cow?
Read Luke 2:6–7.

Baby Jesus was not laid in a cot, but in a manger (a food box for animals).
How does the donkey visit baby Jesus?
Read Luke 2:1–7.

Where was Jesus born?
Which picture of the Bethlehem stable is the odd one out?
Read this story in Luke 2:6–7.

Which box has *all* the pieces needed to make the complete picture of Bethlehem?
Read the story of Jesus' birth in Bethlehem in Luke 2:1–7.

26

Here are six pictures of the story of the birth of Jesus.
Number them in the correct order.
Look at Luke chapters 1 and 2 to help you.

Join up the dots. How many angels can you see now?
Who are the men by the fire?
You can find this story in Luke 2:8–20.

28

These shepherds (and their sheep!) look surprised and happy.
Read Luke 2:8–14 to find out why.
Now use these verses to help you fill in the angel's speech bubble.

These two shepherds are rushing off to Bethlehem to see baby Jesus.
There are twelve differences between the two pictures. Try to find them all!
Read the story in Luke 2:8–20.

Jesus was born in the little town of Bethlehem.
Help the shepherd come to visit baby Jesus.
You can read about this in Luke 2:8–20.

The shepherds rushed to the stable in Bethlehem to see baby Jesus.
They told Mary what the angels had said to them. Join up the dots to complete the picture.
Read the whole story in Luke 2:8–20.

The shepherds visit baby Jesus. Who told the shepherds that baby Jesus had been born?
How many mistakes has the artist made here? Put a circle around every mistake.
This story is in Luke 2:8–20.

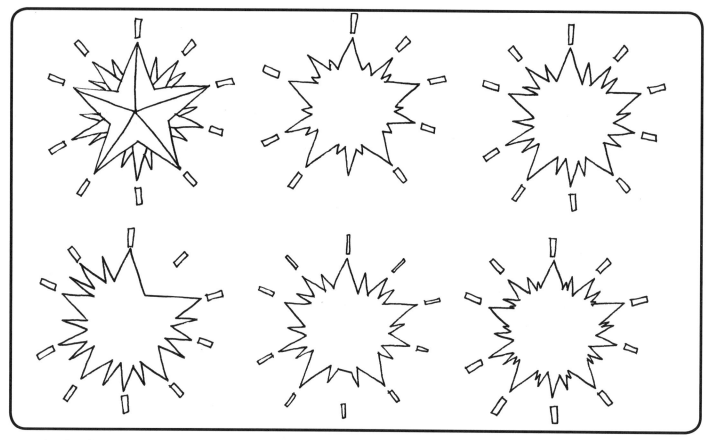

In the East, some wise men were studying the sky. One night they saw a special new star.
They knew that it meant a new king had been born. Which outline exactly fits the finished star?
Read Matthew 2:9–10.

The wise men set off on a long journey, following the star.
Complete this picture with your crayons or felt-tips.
You can read this story in Matthew 2:9–10.

In this picture of the wise men on their journey to find Jesus, the artist has made lots of deliberate mistakes. How many can you find? Should there be two special stars?
Read the story in Matthew 2:1–12.

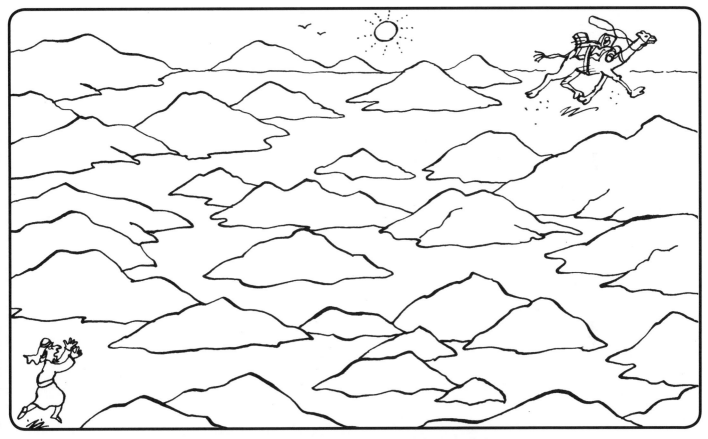

One of the wise men has lost his camel.
Help him track his camel through the maze of sand dunes.
You can read about the wise men in Matthew 2:1–2.

How did the wise men travel?
Join up the dots to find out.
Read this story in Matthew 2:1–2.

Help the wise men find their way across the desert.
Where will they find baby Jesus?
You can read this story in Matthew 2:1–2.

Here are four pictures of a wise man on his camel. Which two are exactly the same?
What did the wise men bring with them for baby Jesus?
Read this story in Matthew 2:1–12.

When the wise men arrived in Jerusalem, they asked King Herod where they would find the newborn king. Finish this picture with your crayons or felt-tips.
You can read this story in Matthew 2:1–12.

King Herod plotted to kill baby Jesus, after the wise men visited him.
Can you find all seventeen stars hidden in this picture?
Look up the story of Herod and the wise men in Matthew 2:1–12.

42

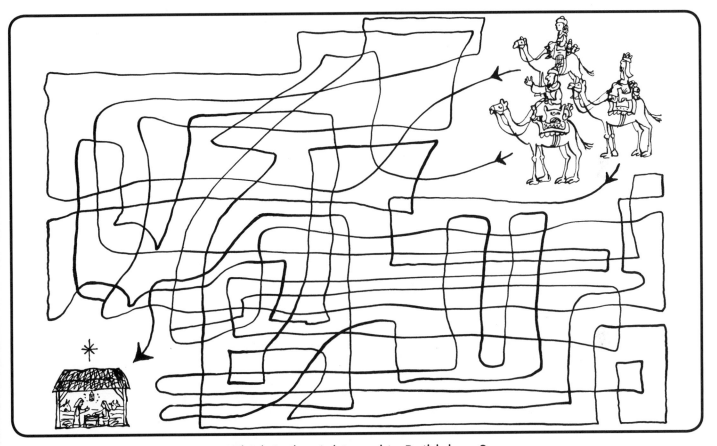

Which is the right road to Bethlehem?
Follow the lines leading from the wise men to find out.
Read the whole story in Matthew 2:1–12.

43

What are the wise men looking at? Join up the dots to find out.
Which town is beneath the star?
Read Matthew 2:1–2.

In this picture of the wise men seeking Jesus, the artist has hidden some stars.
How many can you find?
Read Matthew 2:1–2.

These six drawings of a house in Jesus' time all look the same.
But only two are *exactly* the same. Can you decide which two?
Why did houses in Jesus' time have very small windows?

Help the wise men find the right road from Jerusalem to Bethlehem.
Read Matthew 2:1–12.

The star stopped right over the place where Jesus was.
Can you find ten differences between these two pictures of Bethlehem?
Read the next part of the wise men's story in Matthew 2:9–10.

48

Which gift does each wise man take to Jesus?
Follow the lines to find out.
Read the story of the wise men in Matthew 2:1–12.

49

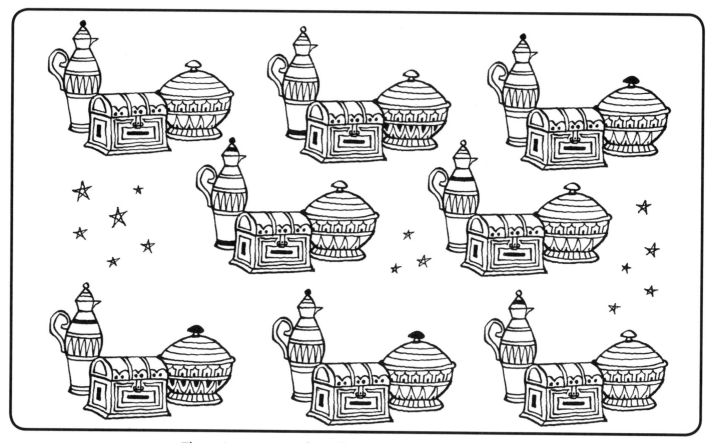

The wise men's gifts. All eight pictures look similar.
Which two pictures are *exactly* the same?
Read the story of the wise men in Matthew 2:1–12.

The wise men found baby Jesus in Bethlehem.
Link the wise men with their gifts. What were their presents?
You can read this story in Matthew 2:1–12.

The wise men all brought a present for baby Jesus.
Complete this picture of the wise men with Mary and Jesus using your crayons or felt-tips.
Read Matthew 2:11 to find out what gifts they brought for him.

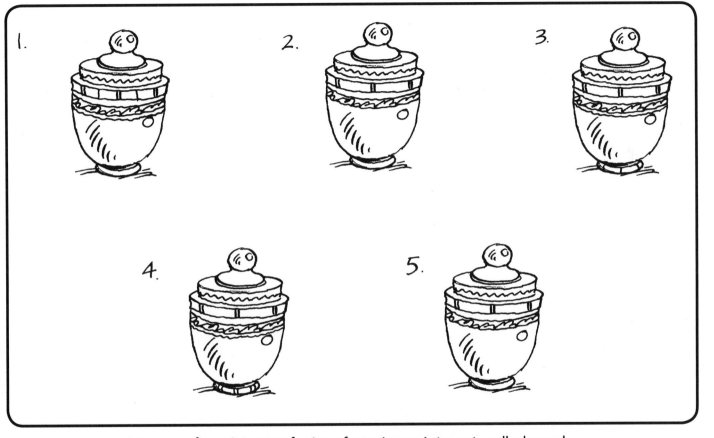

1.

2.

3.

4.

5.

Here are five pictures of a jar of precious ointment, called myrrh.
One of the wise men gave myrrh to baby Jesus. Which two jars are exactly the same?
Read this story in Matthew 2:11.

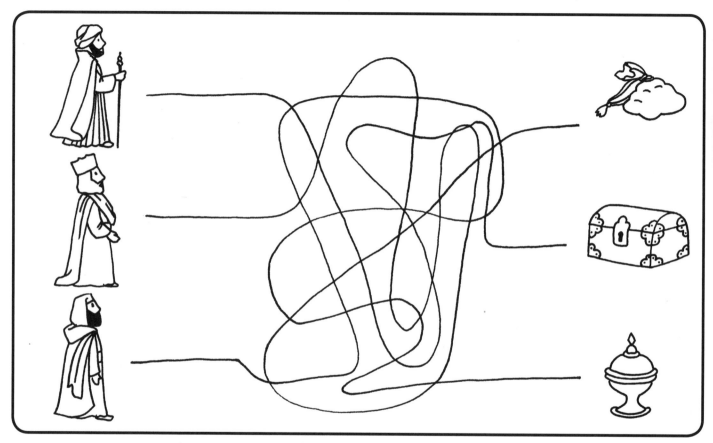

The wise men brought gifts to Jesus. What were they?
Read Matthew 2:11 to find out.
Now join each of the wise men to their presents. Label the gifts.

Mary and Joseph took baby Jesus to the Temple to thank God for him.
An old man called Simeon held the baby. He too thanked God.
Join up the dots to complete the picture. *Read this story in Luke 2:25–32.*

Simeon was a very old man when he saw baby Jesus.
He was happy now, because he had been waiting patiently for Jesus to be born.
Can you find all the mistakes in this picture? *Read about Simeon in Luke 2:22–35.*

Anna was very old too when she saw baby Jesus in the Temple.
How happy she was that this special baby had been born!
Can you find eleven doves in this picture? *Look up the story of Anna's joy in Luke 2:36–38.*

An angel told Joseph it wasn't safe to stay in Bethlehem.
So Joseph took Mary and baby Jesus away to Egypt.
Join up the dots to complete the picture. *Read Matthew 2:13–15.*

58

Can you help Joseph find the road that will take him to safety in Egypt?
Do you know who they are running away from?
Read this story in Matthew 2:13–15.

Perhaps Joseph took Mary and baby Jesus on a donkey when they escaped to Egypt.
Which box has all the pieces to make up the complete donkey?
Read about the escape to Egypt in Matthew 2:13–15.

An angel told Joseph that King Herod wanted to kill baby Jesus. So Mary and Joseph took the baby away to safety in Egypt. *You can read this story in Matthew 2:13.*
Now fill in this illustration with your crayons or felt-tips.

In a dream, God told Joseph it wasn't safe to stay in Bethlehem.
Which path must Mary and Joseph follow to take baby Jesus to Egypt?
This story is in Matthew 2:13–15.

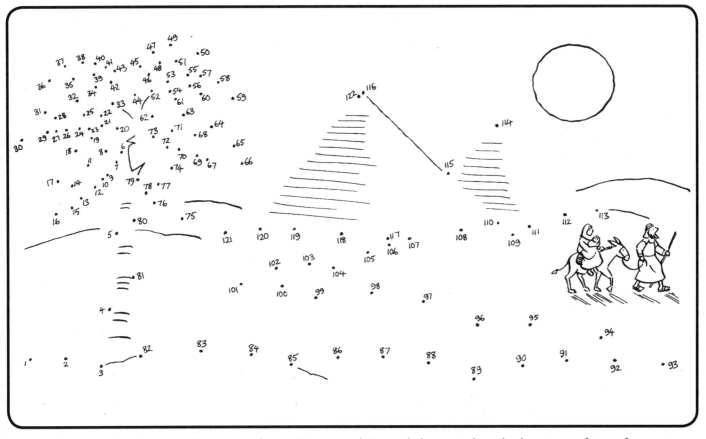

Join up the dots to discover where Mary and Joseph have taken baby Jesus for safety.
Why did they come here?
You can find this story in Matthew 2:13–14.

Here are six pictures of the Christmas story.
Can you number them in the right order?
Look at Luke 2 and Matthew 2 to help you.